A Husband Prays

A Husband Prays

By **ROY G. GESCH**

Concordia Publishing House

St. Louis

Concordia Publishing House, St. Louis, Missouri

© 1968 Concordia Publishing House
Library of Congress Catalog Card No. 68-22574

Second Printing 1970

To Dorothy

who has shown me how wonderful
a good marriage can be

Contents

Preface

To you newlyweds, congratulations!
   To you not so newly wed —
   isn't marriage wonderful?

God has brought you two together. Now it is my prayer that you two may be as one in all your years ahead. With that in mind, this book is offered to you in the hope that it may help to deepen and enrich that oneness.

The first section reminds you of what you have promised to each other and to God when you made your marriage vows. It lets you talk over with God what marriage is intended to be.

The second section is made up of some of the common complaints, the usual trouble spots, that can have a definite effect on marriage — that can either strengthen or weaken the oneness and happiness of it. Since husband and wife do not always see a problem in the same way, a double approach is used, in the hope that it will lead to a discussion of the problem. A deeper appreciation of each other's feelings may be as important as an actual solution. The two companion volumes with identical tables of contents permit individual use, whether you are at home together or separated for a few days.

The topics included have not been drawn blindly. In 20 years of marital counseling, a few

9

things have become apparent. One's own personality traits and attitudes are far more damaging to a marriage than external pressures. There would be fewer divorces, less unhappiness in marriage, less shallowness, if both husband and wife would face up to those potential trouble areas. They may seem trivial and insignificant, but if allowed to grow and become deeply engrained in the fiber of the marriage, they can eventually become great enough to destroy the marriage.

May God bless your marriage!
May He give you a little taste of heaven in it!

ROY G. GESCH

Whittier, California

1
The Essence of Marriage

I Thee Wed

"I take thee to be my wedded wife."

Father, I thank You for making possible
    that unforgettable day
        and the new life that began on that
        day.

I thank You for her
    who has chosen to invest
        her life with mine,
    who has consented
        to bear my name and children.
It seems almost impossible
    that there could be one in this world
        whom I could love so dearly,
        with whom I could be so happy.
I thank You for leading me to her,
    and her to me.

I thank You also, heavenly Father,
    for the wondrous gift of marriage itself.
"It is not good that the man
    should be alone," You said,
        and so You made a fit companion
    that two might be one.

I never cease marveling
    at the uniqueness of this oneness.

Two people —
    so different in every aspect
    yet so compatibly linked to each other,
    each nurturing and furthering the other
        in every way.
For this I thank and praise You, too.

Human minds can reason
    that it is not good for man
        to be alone.
Divine wisdom alone could devise
    the perfectness of marriage
        to meet that need.

Father, let me never take marriage,
    my marriage,
        or my beloved wife
            for granted.
Let me look on them and treat them
    as what they really are —
        priceless gifts of Your understanding
        love.

Hi-Fidelity Promise

"I pledge my faithfulness in every duty."

It was so easy to speak those words, Father,
    to make the promise,

14

when everything had been building up
    to that glorious moment.
I know it is not as easy
    to live that promise
        amidst the trials and perplexities of
        life.
But as sincere as I was in making it,
    so sincere am I in saying
        that, with Your help,
    I will never go back on my word.

Make me faithful, Lord,
    as You are faithful.
"Blessed be the Lord . . .
    Not one word has failed
        of all His good promise."
It's not because it is easier,
    or less costly,
        for You to keep Your word.
Giving up Your Son for me,
    just because You had promised
        to rescue me from the curse of sin,
    is a far greater demand
        than I shall ever have to face.
But despite the personal pain
    You remained true to Your promise
        and true to me.

Make me faithful to my every word, too.
    Let nothing ever happen
        that may even cause my wife to
        wonder

if I have forgotten my vows
   or begun to take them lightly.

There may be many in this world
   who place great importance
      on high fidelity in sound and
         its electronic reproduction
   yet are completely satisfied to have
      low fidelity in marriage.
Let me never become one of them.

Keep me mindful too, Father,
   that I have pledged to be faithful
      "in every duty" —
   not just in things physical or connubial
      but in love, in honor,
         in respect, in consideration.
"Give me a faithful heart" —
   like Yours!

Till Death Us Do Part

"Till death us do part."

Eternal Father, "lifelong"
   may seem like the blink of an eye to
   You,
      who has neither beginning nor end.

But it is a rather unfamiliar quality for us
    who lease-hold Your world
        for a few decades at the most.

Most of what we have and hold
    is ours for such a short time.
We've even grown accustomed to the idea
    of planned obsolescence.
We don't like to say it like this,
    but to a degree our whole economy
        is built on our willingness to waste,
            to outlive, or outgrow.
Even our homes are temporary dwellings.

In contrast to this, Your will in marriage
    is that we should remain one,
        "so long as we both shall live."
Eternal Father, we depend on You
    to enable us to will and to do this.

There are so many dangers and temptations
    to assail the happily married.
Satan doesn't let anyone alone.
    He uses every trick in the bag
        to suggest that a marriage
            has been outgrown
        or that it would be better confiscated
            than remodeled.
Let me never fall prey
    to such deceptive thinking.

The crowning glory of Your promises
    and of Your gracious acts in fulfilling
    them
        is that they are not valid
            only on a limited-time basis;
    I can count on them,
        on my forgiveness and life in Christ,
            as being absolutely certain
        through all of time and eternity.

May such be the crowning glory
    of our marriage too —
the assurance that these joys and blessings
    will not be short-lived
        but will most certainly be ours
            through all our days —
a long-term investment
    that increases in value as it matures
        and will retain its value
            to the very end of our time.

Male and Female

"And God saw everything that He had made,
    and behold, it was very good."

"So God created man . . .
    male and female created He them.
        And behold, it was very good."

"Therefore a man leaves his father and his
mother
      and cleaves to his wife,
          and they become one flesh."
      And behold, it is very good.

Father, fill me with a sense of respect
      and fullest appreciation
          for what You made to be
          so very good.
In a world that tends to distort
      and profane Your wondrous gifts,
          there is temptation for me also,
              even in marriage,
          to look on sex with tongue in cheek.
Help me to accept that intimate oneness
      of man and woman
          from the standpoint
      of what You intended it to be —
      that it may be a time
          of joy and blessing
      rather than an occasion
          for future guilt and remorse.

Father, keep me from becoming a prude,
      for I would thereby be implying
          that Your whole idea
              was not good.
But keep me also from slipping
      into the ever-widening stream of thought
          that excuses obscenity
              as freedom of speech,

that condones promiscuity
as real life,
that applauds entertainment
of low moral tone
as "adult" or "sophisticate."

For, Father, in our moments of intimacy,
and true and complete oneness,
we would enjoy another taste
of the beauty and wonder
of Your creating love
and appreciate the fact
that You made us as we are
and brought us to where we can be
entirely and exclusively for each other.

Leave and Cleave

"A man leaves his father and his mother
and cleaves to his wife,
and they become one flesh."

Lord, teach me how better to deepen
our cleaving to each other.
Sometimes I find myself indulging
in unwarranted critical comparison
that must certainly cut deep —

"It's not the way my mother makes
    it. . . ."
        "My mother . . ."

Lord, help me remember I'm not a little boy
    around the house.
I haven't chosen a younger woman,
        very much to my taste and liking,
            just to be a new mother to me.
I've asked her to be my wife,
        to be completely one with me
            in forming a completely new family
            unit.

Help me to build her up
        and not give her a feeling of inferiority
            by childishly picking away at her
            and attempting to remake her
                in my mother's image.
Help me to see, to respect, and to love her
    for the wonderful person she is.

Teach me also how to stand
        on my own two feet, Lord,
            and not go running back to father
            and mother.
When decisions must be made
    and problems and crises faced,
let me appreciate the counsel and advice
        of those whose greater maturity
            and more diverse experience

has given them a broader perspective
and deeper understanding than my
own.
But help me outgrow the weak tendency
to pass the buck to them,
lest I never fully be a man.

That applies to my relationship
with You too, heavenly Father.
I need to learn to stand
on the strength of my own convictions —
with my two feet firmly planted
on Your Word.
I've all too often let the opinions
and unsolicited ideas of others
get between You and me.

Teach me how to leave others
and to cleave
to my wife
and to You.

That Life May Go On

There are many things in life
that amaze and mystify me, Lord;
though as most become commonplace,
the mystique gradually vanishes.

I marvel at the wonders of electronics,
    the speed of a computer brain,
    the precision of microfilming,
        whereby even the whole Bible
            can be accurately recorded
        on one two-by-two transparency.
I marvel at them, Lord,
    yet even I have the ability to understand
the elemental principles that underlie them.

But I stand in overwhelming awe, Father,
    at the mystery of life.

Day after day babies are born —
    many thousands in every 24-hour period,
        ever since the very beginning.
Billions of living human beings have
experienced
    the miracle of birth,
        of growth, of life.
And I still cannot grasp the "how" of it;
    nor can anyone else to the extent
        where he can imitate
    the creation of life.

"Be fruitful and multiply," You said.
    And therewith You endowed man and woman
        with the wondrous power
            to conceive new life.
You set in motion plans
    whereby one and one could make three,
        and even more;

whereby a man could beget
a son in his image,
different from all others
in that he bears the genetic traits
of those who gave him life.

Father, fill me with the Spirit of Christ,
that I and those whose little feet
shall follow in my footsteps
may be more fully like You,
the Creator and Giver of life,
the Father of us all.

For I realize, Father, that it is not necessary
for me to understand the mystery.
But it is necessary for me
to recognize the responsibilities that are mine
in the ongoing cycle of life.

The Role of a Husband

"Husbands, love your wives."

As those words stand alone, heavenly Father,
I see them as the understatement
of all the aeons of time.

Instead of letting me repeat the words,

"Husbands, love your wives,"
    and then immediately blurt out,
"I do! I love her very much,"
let me see what love should be,
    and examine the love I offer my beloved,
        in the terms You hasten to add.

"Husbands, love your wives"
    as "Christ loved us
        and gave Himself for us."
Love gives!
    Christ loved! Christ gave Himself!
I must practice the art of love
    by giving myself for her
        whom I have asked to be one with me.

But it's so hard, Lord!
    I keep wanting to take all the time.
I keep making demands
    and issuing ultimatums.
I'm always so concerned
    about what I want.

It's hard to give, Lord —
    even courtesy, or kindness,
        or time, or little nothings.
It's even harder to give oneself.
    Yet such is the love I owe.

Teach me how, Lord!
    But then, You have already!

I'm familiar with the perfect sacrifice.
    But it's not a simple pattern.
I could never fully attain the love
    Christ's giving involved.

I'm thankful that You also said,
    "Let each one of you love his wife
        as himself."
Now I'm back to where
    I can use my feelings, my desires,
        my needs, and my concerns
    as a basis of judgment;
        and these I can understand.
Yes, Lord, I know I must care for her
    as if she were my own life, my own body.
That's what Christ did for us.
Help me see that's what love is all about.

The Role of a Wife

How often I have teased, Father,
    about the promise my beloved wife
        made in the wedding ceremony.
At the proper moment I've reminded her,
    "You promised to obey."
But she has always been fully aware
    that I really understand
        both the intent and the extent
            of that word.

I do realize, dear Lord,
  that a wife does have obligations
    to her husband and to her family.
But I realize also
  that they have a direct relationship
    to the husband's living up to
      his end of the pact.

As we are subject to Christ,
  "so let wives . . . be subject in everything
    to their husbands."
This is the message of Your Word.
Love begets love.
  We love Him who first loved us.
    We serve Him who served us
      both in life and death.

I pray therefore, Father,
  that I may so love
    and live for my wife,
  that her natural response
    may be a deep love for me
  and the desire to live for me.

You also stated: "Let the wife see
  that she respects her husband."
Father, make me the kind of man
  whom she can truly respect.

I know there are times —
  and I ask Your and her forgiveness —

when I act like a tinhorn sergeant,
a chaise-lounge dictator
barking out orders
and criticisms indiscriminately.
Help me to see that love and respect
are not gained in such a manner.

Fill me with the desire
and the willingness to be more like Christ
in my attitudes and acts towards her.
For only then can there be good reason
why she should be filled with love for me.

Divorce?

What's wrong with us, Lord?
Why do we so often
abuse Your good gifts,
and try to get around
what we know is right?
It is asked, now as then,
"Is it lawful to divorce
one's wife for any cause?"
Even though Jesus stated clearly,
"What God has joined together,
let no man put asunder,"

there are almost as many divorces
    as there are marriages.

Every day, Lord,
I hear or read of people asking,
    "What are legitimate grounds?"
It's obvious they are only looking for
    the legal loophole,
        the easy way out,
    not a way to make something good
        out of their marriage.

Lord, help us to cherish our marriage
    and each other.
Should we feel there are deficiencies
    in our life together,
give us wisdom to build better
    rather than just destroy.

Give us mature minds,
    that we may not be overgrown babies,
        bawling loudly to get our own ways,
        or running away from it all.

I know that a person can find an excuse
    for almost anything anytime.
Excuses bring to light
    what a man really wants
    and what he's really like.

A person can also find reasons and excuses
    why a marriage might not work.

But Lord, isn't it our job
    to make it work?
    to make of it something
        truly happy and blessed?

Fill us with that earnest will.
Impart to us Your power,
    Your wisdom, and Your love,
that our home may be ever
    strong and good.

2
Live-a-Day Problems

Appearance

Lord, I think once in a while
    about this whole business
        of personal appearance.

When I get together with people
    who might affect my future,
        I go all out to impress them.
When I go to church,
    I try to look my Sunday best —
        in clothes, bearing, demeanor,
            even in language.

What I wonder at times is:
    Am I really that way?
    Or is it just an appearance?

If I know what is desirable,
    enough to be that way publicly,
        why am I content to be
            less than that at home?

"A man's home is his castle,"
    we like to say,
"If I can't be myself at home,
    where can I?"

But Lord, if being myself means
      being insensitive to my wife's feelings,
            even discourteous or inconsiderate,
      or setting up an image
            less than what I admire
                  or respect in others,
I'm not so sure then, Lord,
      that I should want to be myself.

But why should it be so?

It's not that I feel
      that now the chase is over —
            just to have my wife is enough —
nor that others play a more important role
      in my life than my own family.
It's more that I just don't think.

Help me, Lord, to be the man
      I try so hard to appear to be.

When I come to you in worship,
      I try to reflect the spirit of Christ.
It's no act!
      That's how I want and pray to be.
Lord, make me that way!
      Everywhere! Also at home!

Communication

Father, I talk so much all day —
  commuting to and from work,
  while I'm on the job,
  at coffee breaks,
  and during lunch hours —
that often I forget
  that talking and communicating
  are not always the same thing.

It's the same old pattern day after day —
  either the normal business jargon
    or the usual idle banter,
  sharp criticism I would like to forget
    but remember,
  a good joke I would like to remember
    but forget.

So much talk, so little said!
  So many words, so few thoughts, concerns,
    dreams, or convictions really shared!
Father, don't let that become my pattern of speech
  or my way of thinking or living.

When I am at home with my wife
  and when I'm alone with You,
    let me communicate, not just talk.

Let my words be like drapes thrown open wide
    to allow my loved ones — and that includes
    You —
            to see into the windows of my heart and
            mind.
Use my words to
    bring about that togetherness
        that is more than just being together.

Father, as I ask this of You,
    I know You can make it possible.
I marvel at how You have communicated
    Your love and Your truth to us.
You gave us words —
            expressing depths of thought and love
                that stagger even my imagination;
    words —
        providing answers to my hazy
            and not fully formulated questions;
    words —
        guiding, teaching,
            giving peace and hope.
And, aware of the weakness of words,
    the way they invite misunderstanding,
You gave us Christ the living Word
    who cannot be misunderstood,
            through whom I know, believe,
            and rejoice in Your forgiving and saving
            love.

36

Father, help me communicate my love
    to those who need my love,
        as I need to know theirs.

Togetherness

Heavenly Father, it is apparent
    that to promote and maintain oneness,
        which is the heart of marriage,
    togetherness is required.

It also becomes increasingly apparent
    that true togetherness means more than
        living in the same house,
        eating at the same table,
        sleeping in the same bed.

It's more than
    planning a joint budget,
    living off one income,
    fretting over the same bills.

Togetherness must involve also
    our dreams, our hopes, our plans,
and our working together
    to make them materialize.

Father, make us sensitive
    to each other's joys and tears,
    aware of each other's feelings.

Give us also the joy
    of sharing our faith with each other,
that we can be one
    in worship and prayer,
        at home and at church.

You deemed it important enough
    to urge that we strive,
        even outside the home,
    to keep a true spiritual oneness
        "in the bond of peace."
If it is important that we,
    in our relations with others,
        strive for "one hope, one Lord,
            one faith, one baptism,"
surely it's doubly significant
    in the togetherness
        that is ours at home.

Give us true togetherness, Father,
    and the peace and strength
        that flow from it.

And grant us wisdom
    that You may ever be a part
        of that togetherness.

Pastime and Recreation

Father, why is it that two people
    who try to make a good life together,
who share goals, principles, and ideals,
    may suddenly decide
        to go separate ways
    where fun is concerned?

In days of courtship
    they were inseparable.
They spent every possible moment
    with each other.
They laughed together
    and played together.
Their mutual enjoyment
    was one of the prime factors
that led them to the desire and decision
    to spend all of life together.

How then can it change
    when the two become one?

What has happened
    when suddenly it seems to be more fun
        to be out with the boys,
    and enjoyable family outings
        become less frequent?

Must it not mean that,
        at least to a degree,
love has given way to selfishness?

Father, I know it is inevitable
        that each have personal preferences,
                even after getting married.
One really enjoys sports —
        another concerts and plays.
One likes to relax at home —
        another to go out and do things.

But can't we concede
        and adjust to each other?
Can't we share each other's pleasure?
        Isn't that a part of love?
Help us to find the way.

It's often been said, Father, that
        "Families that pray together
                stay together."
I believe this is true.
But I believe there is some truth also in
        "Families that play together
                stay together."

Slow Us Down, Lord!

We live at such an accelerated pace,
    that we don't know what to do
    when someone suddenly jams on the brakes.
Slow us down, Lord!

We become so obsessed
    with the forward surge,
        the pace we set,
        the ground we cover,
    that we lose sight
        of the wonder and beauty
            of where we are.

Make me mindful
    of our daily blessings, Lord!
Let not my quest for castles
    cause me to overlook
        the warmth and peace and strength
        of our very own home.
Let not my elation
    in meeting and hobnobbing
        with men of fame and stature
    cause me to minimize the worth
        of that most personal relationship
        that is our very own.

I've seen so many caught up
    in heady exhilaration,
        so impressed with where they were going.

They weren't prepared
    for any possible screeching halt,
        yet it came!
And they ended up
    bruised and shaken —
        losers from every point of view.
What they had
    they were willing to let slip away,
        gambling for what they might have.
Now they have nothing.

Slow us down, Lord, now!
Now, before our flame becomes an ember.
Now, before our children
    grow up and away from us.

Give us the wisdom to take time
    for each other.
Give us the wisdom to take time
    for You, Lord.

For even a pinnacle
    can be a lonely, tragic place,
        when you've left your loved ones behind.

Money

Father, would it be wrong if,
    here and now, I prayed for money?

Money does play rather prominently
    in our thinking.
One of the first things a man asks
    when he considers a new job is
        "What is the salary?"
And money is a prime reason
    why some of us continue to work.
We would rather retire early.

So, Father, when in all honesty
    we work hard for our money
        and plan accordingly,
    shouldn't we also pray for it?

Isn't money a part of the good things
    that You bestow on us?
Haven't You said that "the love of money
    is the root of all evil"?
Not "money" — the "love of money."

Can I not therefore pray for money
and at the same time pray
    to be kept from "the love of money"?

Father, give us what we really need
        and whatever extra You know
            to be for our good.

Give us also the ability
        to use it well.
Don't let us squander selfishly
        on waste and frippery,
while we begrudge the alms
        to alleviate others' needs.
The sparkle of diamonds is tawdry
        compared with the sparkle
            in appreciative eyes.
The thrill of having soon fades,
        but the joy that comes with sharing
            is constantly multiplied.

You gave us the Best,
        instead of saving it for Self.
Mountains of gold and silver
        could not mean to us
what Christ means or His sacrifice.

So, Father, as we deal
        in terms of worth and cost,
            help us to evaluate properly.
Let our goal be not what we have
        but how we use it,
and therein find Your blessing.

Trust and Jealousy

Dear Lord, I know that trust is essential
    to every happy marriage.
There's not much of a healthy future
    if either husband or wife
    is the kind that harbors suspicion
        that imagines the worst
        the moment the other is out of sight.

No, I'm not so naive, Lord,
    as to think that jealousy
        is always out of place.
You had good reason
    for asserting, time and again,
"I, the Lord your God,
    am a jealous God!"

Why shouldn't You be —
    when the glory due You
        is directed elsewhere?
    when the love due You
        is coldly withheld?
You have full cause to remind that
    You made us,
    You rescued us
        from the destructive power of sin,
    You worked out our unending good.
We are truly Yours.
    We owe You life and all.

We owe each other a lot
    in our marriage, too.
We've promised lifelong love
    and wholehearted fidelity.
If the promise be broken —
    yes, there's cause for jealousy!
        Good cause!

But, Lord, don't let that happen to us!
Keep us so close to each other
    in mind and spirit
that there is not even the temptation
    to distrust the other
        when we are apart.
Fill us with that peaceful confidence
    that comes with knowing
that we think more of each other
    than anyone else
        in this whole wide world.

Forgive

Lord Jesus, why do I find it
    so hard to forgive?

You could call Judas "Friend,"
    when You saw the kiss of death on his lips.
You could ask Peter how much he loved You,
    so soon after he had publicly disclaimed You.
You could "die for us
    while we were yet sinners."
You could love us enough
    to sacrifice Yourself completely for us,
        before we even came pleading for Your
        help.

Why then, Lord Jesus,
    when I so appreciate forgiveness,
        and so rejoice in being forgiven,
    do I find it so difficult to forgive —
        even those I love the most?

There are bound to be moments of difference,
    ill-chosen words, heightened emotions.
        After all, nobody's perfect.
But all too often my temper flares,
    and she sits in teary-eyed silence —
both feeling wronged,
    both waiting for the other to apologize.
Why, Lord?

I know You have said:
    "Be kind to one another,
        forgiving one another,.
    as God in Christ forgave you."

That's just the way I want to be,
    especially at home.
Yet sometimes it is there
    that I carry my grudge the longest.

Lord Jesus, fill our hearts with Your love!
Keep me aware of my shortcomings,
    my stubbornness, my inconsiderateness,
        and how they must both hurt
            and irritate my loved ones,
that I may also be aware
    of how hard it must be for them
        to forgive me every day.
Perhaps the demands on my forgiving love
    may be very small in contrast.

Keep me aware of the price You paid
    to bring about my forgiveness.
Give me also such an overriding love, Lord!

Dreams and Plans

Lord, I thank You for today.
I also thank You for tomorrow.

Not because tomorrow
    is an extension of today
but because tomorrow,
    and other tomorrows to follow,
offer unlimited opportunity
    to plan and dream.

If You, by bringing us together,
    could make our today so great,
what eager hope
    can we not rightly hold
        for tomorrow?
For You, who have blessed
    both past and present,
will be with us
    in our future, too.

We thank You, Lord,
    "for You are good,
    for Your mercy endures forever."

I'm Tired!

I'm tired, Lord Jesus!

Sometimes I get to feeling so beat,
    I just want to run away from it all.

You know how it feels!
    When I see the frightful pressures
        under which You lived,
    I wonder how You could possibly
        stand up under it.

But perfect love caused You, Lord Jesus,
    no matter how tired You were,
to take little ones in Your arms
    and bless them;
to take the burdens and cares
    of all who cried in hope
as an even trade for Your merciful love.

There were times, though,
    when You retreated.
        Weren't there, Lord?
Not as a means of withdrawing
    but to gain renewed strength,
You went into the mountains,
You shoved off from shore,
You slipped into the Garden
    to pray and rest.

I notice too how You
    sought out Your loved ones
        for those quiet hours —
Your heavenly Father
    and those particularly close to You.

Lord Jesus, we've been told:
    "Be not weary in well-doing."
How much I want it to be that way.
But I still end up so often
    so depressed, so tired,
        so ready to shut it all out
    when I want to be more like You.
Make me wise enough
    to see I need moments of retreat,
        moments when I can be alone.
Alone — yet with You
    and with my loved ones.

Strengthen me through such moments
    of prayer and rest and peace.

Thus I can face the tasks
    of another day
and still be fresh enough
    to let love have its full way.

Temper! Temper!

Lord, You see into every heart and mind.
You've seen how hard I have to struggle
    to hold my temper at times.
Those who casually window-shop my features
    see the well-groomed smile.
But You and I know how often
    I am seething inside.

What troubles me so deeply
    is that my family usually gets the brunt
        of my short-fused explosions.
The ones I love most I hurt most.
Yet even as I angrily cut them down
    with vicious use of tongue,
        I know they deserve it least.

Lord, I know I can control myself.
I do at work —
    lest I lose my position.
I do with friends —
    lest they think ill of me.
Yet often it's there,
    at work or with friends,
that I have most cause to feel enraged.

Then I come home,
    and the slightest spark sets me off.

I know that what I'm really doing
    is lashing out at them
because of the anger I feel towards others.
    Help me change, Lord!

Give me the courage
    to voice my displeasure
        to those who have it coming.
Give me the ability, likewise,
    to hold my tongue,
        to think and pray before I speak,
    when it has to do with
        the minor irritants in our home.

Let me learn of You, Lord God.
    Your Word states pointedly:
"The wrath of God is revealed from heaven
    against all ungodliness
        and wickedness of men."

That's just the point, Lord!
    You are angry when there is just cause
        for You to be angry,
    and it's specifically at those
        who give rise to that anger.
Otherwise You are all grace, mercy, and love.
Teach me Your way, O Lord!

Honesty

"All the world's a stage," it is said.

Lord, I hate to think that everyone
    is just putting on an act.
Surely someone is sincere
    and truly being himself.
Surely some of our contacts
    are dealing with us honestly.

Sincerity and honesty are so necessary
    in all of life.
There's such heartache
    in the letdown of deceit.
I remember how You lamented those
    who honored You with lips and mouth,
    while their hearts were far from You.
These were people of whom
    You had reason to expect more.
Really, that's where dishonesty shows up
    in its worst ugliness —
there, where true love should reign.

Lord, let me be consistently open and honest
    with my family above all.
Dare I whisper,
    "I love you, darling!"
and then turn right around
    and work behind her back?

Sometimes I've made the mistake
    of concealing little things.
"There's no point in telling!
    I'll shield her," I've reasoned.
I didn't want her to see
    how foolish I was
    or how I failed.
I wanted her to look up to me
    with respect as well as love.

But, Lord, doesn't it always backfire?
When she discovers I've lied,
    where then is respect?
What reason should she have
    to trust me in anything?

It means so much to me to know
    that all You've said is true.
I can believe it, without trying
    to read between the lines
    or seeking hidden implication.

Father, make me a man of truth,
    a man of honesty and sincerity!

The Gift of Understanding

Lord God, give me the ability to understand —
    especially my wife.

At times I feel rather frustrated.
I can find a very logical solution
    to some of our besetting problems,
then suddenly I run into emotion and intuition,
    which seem more valid to her.

We're both earnestly looking for an answer.
    But we go at it in such different ways.
Give me enough understanding
    that I may see the good in this.

You, Father, did not make us identical.
You willed that we should be compatible.
    And this is good!

We are to complement each other,
    offset each other
        and compensate for each other.
For we truly need each other.

Should I see weakness in her,
    let me not criticize
        but supply the wanted strength.

Should I feel riled up and hurt
    and nurse my wounds in self-pity,
let me be grateful to have a wife
    whose soothing love
        can snap me out of it.

Give us love and understanding
    such as Yours for us.
You've always had reason
    to be disappointed in us,
        and to criticize us sharply.
Yet You've always offered to atone,
    not reject.
In Christ You've provided
    strength for our weakness,
    hope for our despair,
    pardon and peace for our sinfulness,
    a future with promise.
Always of Your fullness
    You've made up for our emptiness.
For You understand our need
    and have the love and power to provide.

Give us the same, O Lord!

On Getting Ahead

Father, I have an overwhelming desire
    to get ahead.
Position, status, income,
    all have one common characteristic —
    the more you have, the more you want.

Once I just worked towards advancement;
        now I have a constantly increasing desire
            to go all the way to the top.
Once I pushed for a slightly larger paycheck,
    to be able to pay off my juggled bills;
            now even my much-multiplied salary
    won't keep pace with my fanciful imagination.
Once I wanted others just to treat me as an equal;
    now I find myself bypassing others
            without extending even the time of day.

It's so hard, Father,
    once you get caught up in the game,
        to play it Your way.
"There is great gain in godliness
    with contentment," You say.
I know and believe that, Father,
    but it's hard to practice it
        when you're living in a competitive
        world.

I'm asking You, Father,
　　to regulate my desires and ambitions,
　　　　as all of my life,
　　by Your discerning will.
By Your will You gave me life;
　　through Christ You redeemed my life
　　　　and called me as Your very own.
I know You want only my good.

I realize that high ground
　　makes one more vulnerable to potshots
and that a red carpet
　　can be pulled out from under you
　　　　as easily as any other.
But Father, if it be Your will
　　that I be advanced to high places,
give me the wisdom, integrity, and courage
　　necessary to match the position;
　　　　and protect me and my family
　　from the many obvious pitfalls.

If You see fit, Father,
　　to place material wealth into my hands,
give me with it the kind of perspective
　　that will enable me to manage it
　　　　as a means for what is truly good,
　　also in accord with Your will.

Thin Skins

Lord, of all the anatomical problems
    that plague the human race
few are as aggravating as
    having too thin a skin.

Weak knees, stiff necks,
    cold feet, hot heads,
all wreak their share of havoc.
But there is generally a way
    to avoid or compensate.

But when two lives
    are joined so closely,
hypersensitivity
    can be an irritating thing.
We're bound to bump into and
    rub each other the wrong way
        once in a while.

Lord, enable us to walk
    in step with each other,
avoiding jarring clash
    by the very harmony
        of movement and direction.

Lord, enable us also to walk
    side by side.

For so our eyes are not riveted
    on each other's faults and flaws.

Keep us conscious, Lord,
    especially when our thin skins smart,
how much reason You have
    to feel hurt with us.
You've found it in Your heart
    to forgive.
Can we do less?

Language

"With the tongue
    we bless the Lord and Father,
and with it we curse men.
From the same mouth
    come blessing and cursing.
This ought not to be so."

The male interest
    in tools and weapons
should make me conscious
    of the harm that can be done
        by their careless use.

The tongue is both
    tool and weapon.

Words can build or destroy,
    bolster or belittle,
        soothe or slash.
Father, make me responsible
    in the use of my tongue.

Seal my lips to profane
    or blasphemous speech
or anything else that suggests
    lovelessness to You
        or to my loved ones.

Remind me that my words
    as well as my actions
are affecting other lives
    and shaping younger minds.

Make me aware that
    all words and actions
are display windows,
    through which attitudes
        are clearly seen.
To hem and haw,
    "I didn't really mean it!"
does not undo an unfortunate display.
    Impressions remain.

Father, make me master
    of my tongue and mind.
May what I say
    and what I am
conform to Your good will.

Daily Tasks

I've often looked at snow-crowned mountain
peaks
    with longing, Lord.
But when I had scaled the heights
    and stood there alone
        in the icy wind,
the lush green valleys below,
    whence I came,
looked mighty warm and inviting.

Sometimes I look at the lives of others
    and I regret
        that mine is so very ordinary.
There are men in conquest
    and others who describe their exploits
        with exciting words.
There are those who play
    at sport on field
and others who play
    at life on stage.
There are those who make their living
    traveling, researching,
        studying, exploring.
And I?

No, I'm not complaining, Lord.
    I'm sure others are attracted
    to my comparatively simple life
        and my home and family.

Though my daily tasks may tend to be
    routine and tedious,
they have their importance too.

There was no glamor in the cross.
Caesar was the object of public envy;
Pilate commanded the legions;
Caiaphas manipulated the church;
But Jesus redeemed the world.

He prayed unnoticed in the garden.
He was rejected by the in-crowd.
He died as a human discard.
Yet so He served,
    and so He saved us all.

Mine is quite a different task,
    yet therein I also serve.
Help me to do it well.
Let me see that even little things
    have big worth
        when they are done rightly.

Work Obligations

I've heard it said, Father:
> "I'm married to the Marine Corps first . . ."
> "I'm married to my work."

What's usually implied is that
> someone deserves a good pat on the back.

Oh, sure, we all admire
> hard work and stick-to-itiveness
> > when we see it in a person,
> and we should respect and commend him
> > for real dedication.

The world would be a lot better off
> if there were more dedicated men,
> > more willing to put themselves out
> > > to get a job done well.

I want to be that way myself.

There is no better pattern than Christ!
His dedication never ran out.
> His loving service knew no bounds.

But I can't forget that Jesus was working
> at something of unquestionable worth.

I see a world of difference
> between man's eternal redemption
> > and the tasks we tackle each day.

Father, I don't like the way
> the phrase "married to"
> > is bandied about so loosely.

When one then is "married to" his job
    and gives that preference to family,
isn't that a kind of adultery all its own?

Father, I ask for interest in my work,
    readiness to give it my very best,
    satisfaction in seeing worthy accomplishment.

But Father, I ask also that I may never,
    because of work or other consideration,
relegate my family
    to a position of minor importance.

I am one of many at work.
    Sickness and death soon enough prove
how dispensable the individual is
    in the organization.

My position in my home is unique;
    my wife has no other husband —
        my children no other father.
Don't let me minimize
    my place or my responsibilities there.

Help me do a really good job at work.
    But let me be "married to" my family.

The Business Trip

"It is not good that the man should be alone."
It's funny Father, how fully Your words,
    spoken so very long ago,
        apply to a business trip.

A man alone . . .
It's not so bad in the daytime,
    when you make your contacts
    and attend your conferences.
It's the evenings.

Meals are soon eaten and records entered.
    Then what? A man alone!

Oh, there's plenty of chance
    to have a good time.
Someone always knows the place
    to grab a few short ones,
        though they're never few or short.
Someone's always there to remind
    that no one knows you in this town,
so here's the chance to take in a show
    you wouldn't dare go see at home.
And someone always knows
    some girls that would be good company —
        just for a few innocent laughs.
A man alone . . .
    In a rented room, in a strange town.

Television? Movie? Oh, it helps.
But it's not the same when you're alone.
Usually there's a Bible
    in the dresser drawer,
one that looks as if no one
    has ever opened it.
I've heard of people
    who let it fall open,
and their eyes rested on words
    that changed their whole lives.
Nothing like that happens to me.
But I do read,
    and I do get some good from it.

Be with me, Father!
There's always the temptation
    to let down a little
        when one is all alone.
Keep me strong!

"I need Thy presence
    every passing hour.
What but Thy grace
    can foil the Tempter's power?"

I'm Bored!

I'm bored, Lord!
    Routine has its way
        of getting under one's skin.

I shouldn't be!
    I should be thankful
        that I have a job,
            an unlimited future,
        health to do my work,
            and loved ones
        with whom to share all.
And I am thankful to You, Lord,
    for blessing me so!

I guess I'm a lot like
    the children of Israel —
    a free people, with a future,
        on their way to their own land,
    fed and guided by You.
Yet after a stint of wandering,
    prolonged by their own halfheartedness,
they're ready to trade off
    Your promise and their hopes and dreams
        for a little of the old way,
            futureless though it be.

Oh, there is monotony in our lives!
The unfailing daily paper
    has unfailingly similar news.
I see the same faces,
    day in, day out,
anticipate the same greetings,
    perform the same tasks,
hear the same pep talks —
    there's so much always the same.
No wonder one dreams
    of slipping off alone,
    of tropical islands,
    of retiring at 35.

But Lord, help me see purpose
    and reason in what I do.
Let me see how I am serving and
    whom I am serving.
Jesus bore pain
    in serving those He loved.
Let me be willing to endure boredom
    for those I love.

Selfishness

Lord Jesus, it bothers me —
    though surely not enough —
that a person can think
    so much of himself and
    so little of others.

Why should You have had to say:
    "Thou shalt love thy neighbor
        as thyself"?

I know what You mean, Lord.
    I love myself — we all do!
If we would care for others
    the way we take care of ourselves,
how much better this world would be.

But Lord, if You ask this
    of me with my neighbor,
what of me with my wife?

"Nourish her
    and cherish her," You said,
"as if she were your own body."

O Lord, what I can easily understand
    I have trouble doing.
It seems so normal
    to think of myself first.

But where then is love?
    Where oneness?

Help me to catch
    Your spirit of love,
to put her first,
    as You put us first:
to be more concerned about her needs
    than I am about mine.

For such is Your way, Lord!
    Such should mine be!

One in Faith

"You'd better go to church
    without me today!
I have too much to do!"

I know better than that, Father!

Yet how often I've found
    and used a convenient excuse
to pass up opportunities
    to be with my family and You
        in worship.

I've heard it said that some men
        send a family delegate,
        someone to represent them all
            at church each Sunday.
I've also heard the hard-hitting
        and keen-cutting parody:
"Take my wife, and let her be
Consecrated, Lord, to Thee."

But, Father, You know
        I don't feel that way.
Forgive me when my weakness of flesh
        causes me to neglect Your Word.

Jesus promised:
        "Blessed are they
            that hear the Word of God and keep it."

Father, I need such blessing!
I need daily strength,
        guidance, and assurance.
I need both anchorage
        and uplift.
I need Your Word,
        as I need daily food.
I therefore earnestly desire to hear
        and keep Your Word.

Make me more like Joshua.
"As for me and my house," he declared,
        "we will serve the Lord."
He didn't let it go with himself.

He took the initiative
for the whole family.
He was concerned that they be one in faith and
that they together serve the Lord.

Make me a man of faith, Father!
Make me strong enough spiritually
to lead my loved ones to You and
to strengthen them
by the power of Christian example.
Through the years let us sit side by side,
hearing of our Savior's love,
and as we move
actively carrying out His will.

Breadwinning

Heavenly Father I thank You
for the health to work
and a job to do
and the ability thereby to provide
for the material needs of my family.

"In the sweat of your face
you shall eat bread," You foretold.
I've learned that sweat wipes off
and aching muscles soon relax
when one has food to eat
and a grateful heart.

Father, help me to carry out my daily tasks
    without grumbling and complaining,
lest I give cause for needless concern
    to my loved ones at home.

I treasure their confidence.
    It does my heart good to see my loving wife
        manage the affairs of the family
    without first double-checking to see
        if I will work to provide for tomorrow.

Oh, there are times, Father,
    when I begrudge the burden —
        You know that as well as I!
    Bread without sweat —
        either mental or physical —
            can sound pretty appealing.

When such times come,
    let my calm dependence on You
        show forth more fully.
Enable me then to pray, as Jesus did,
    "Father, if You are willing,
        remove this . . . . Nevertheless . . . ."
Jesus found strength to rise
    and finish His task
    of loving and redeeming the mankind
        He came to save.
I know renewed strength
    and willingness will come to me, too,
        as I see again the importance of working
        and what it means to those I love.

Father, give me ever the quiet assurance that
    "You open Your hand and satisfy
        the desire of every living creature."

A Sense of Humor

Father, there's so much
    that's right and good in life
that we have reason to be
    very happy people.

Oh, there are occasional clouds
    that obscure the brightness,
        but they soon scud away.

Lord, help us keep
    a good sense of humor.
Where love reigns, a smile
    should be the order of the day.
When someone mopes and droops
    around the house a lot
or clams up in utter silence,
    it's bound to rub off.

But a light heart and bright smile
    are contagious, too.
They make everything seem
    so much more worthwhile.

You said in Proverbs:
    "A cheerful heart is a good medicine."
That's true! Our problems fade out
    much more quickly
        when we do not lose
    our sense of humor over them.

Really, Lord, I think
    humor is one of the best tools You put
        into our working kit.
I don't mean the ability to tell a joke
    or to remember funny stories
but the ability to laugh,
    to laugh at ourselves,
to be genuinely cheerful and happy.
If we didn't know You,
    Your power or Your love,
if we didn't have hope
    and life in Christ,
there would be much reason
    for long faces.

But we do!
    Let our daily happiness
        reflect our trust
        and our love for You
            and each other!

Sharing Responsibility

"Honey, when are you going to mow the lawn?"
    "The kitchen faucet is leaking!"

How irritating that can be
    at times, heavenly Father.
After a fellow has worked
    pretty hard all day
and fought traffic
    all the way, both ways,
he looks forward to the peace of home
    and enjoying his family —
not just being a handyman around the house.

I'm pretty tired when I get home.
    Now I'm supposed to do more?
        Isn't one job enough?
Or am I being shortsighted?
I know well enough that
    when my wife has the know-how,
she tackles all the upkeep
    and minor repairs she can,
        just so I do not have to.
It's so easy to overlook the fact
    that she has borne her share
        of the load, too,
            all day long.

There's always such a temptation
    to push things off on others.
Home is not immune from it either.
And when something isn't quite right,
    it's so easy to say:
"It wouldn't have happened
    if you had done your part."

Lord, make each of us willing
    to shoulder fully
        our individual responsibilities.
Give us also the feeling
    that we are helping each other.

I want to do my part!
    No, Father! More than that!
I've rarely seen anybody
    who is obsessed with the idea
that he wants to do his part —
    but only his part! —
        even go halfway.

Give me more of the Spirit of Christ!
Love moved Him
    to assume responsibility
        that was not His.

"Surely He has borne our griefs
    and carried our sorrows."
There was no reason He had to.
    It was our responsibility.

After all, are they not our griefs,
    our sorrows, our burdens, our sin?
Should not we bear them —
    blame, penalties, and all?

But He did it!
And by it He assured our salvation.

Father, give me also such love
    to do my part and even more.

Social Status

Father, I keep telling myself that
    in this fair and free land of ours
        there is no caste system.
Yet I am always conscious
    that many are almost obsessed
to move up to a better neighborhood,
to meet and mix with the right people,
to keep up with the Joneses
    in an ostensible way.

I suppose everyone has some feeling
    of wanting to be accepted,
especially by the ones who have made it,
    of wanting to be a part of the in-crowd,
    of wanting to be on the top of the heap.

But I hear Jesus hauntingly ask,
    "What will it profit a man
        if he gains the whole world
    and forfeits his life?"
The price is too great!
Gain is no gain
    if the loss is greater.
Father, don't ever let my sense of values
    get so unbalanced
        that I end up a loser.

I know that my human ambition
    will never cease, Father.
Nor would I want it to.
Goals and objectives
    add zest to life.

But let me give You
    more of a free hand
        in shaping these goals
    in my life.
Let my desire to be "in"
    be to be "in" with You.
Let me never forget
    that Your blessings
        are my greatest wealth.
Keep me mindful that
    the highest position of all comes
        when I wear the crown of life,
which I know is already mine in Christ.

Impatience

Make me a patient man, O Lord!
Does not waiting
    whet the appetite
        and sweeten the taste?
Anticipation serves well
    to heighten the joy
        of fulfillment.

Is not this also the mark
    of a mature mind?
I can understand
    and chuckle at the child
who, squirming in the back seat
    through the first half hour
        of a 500-mile trip,
asks impatiently,
    "Are we almost there, Daddy?"
But dare I go through life
    like that?
Can I not find peace
    in accepting Your time
        and Your way
            and Your measure?

And Lord, make me
    patient with others.
Sometimes I expect too much
    of others

without ever realizing it.
Since I am not a perfect being,
    do not let me demand
        perfection in others.

Keep me mindful that if ever one had cause
    to be impatient, it is You, Lord!
Not because there is much we cannot do;
but because we do not do what we can —
because we have fallen so far
    from Your image.

Yet, Lord Jesus,
    You did not turn against us.
You loved us all the same —
    and still do!
What was lacking You supplied.
Where we failed, You succeeded
    on our behalf.

Blessed Lord! Give me
    a measure of Your patience.

Taking Each Other for Granted

What was it Paul wrote?
'In everything by prayer
    and supplication with thanksgiving

let your requests be made known
    to God."

Lord Jesus, impress on me
      the importance of that phrase,
        "with thanksgiving."
It's so easy to take
    everything for granted —
Your love,
    the privilege of prayer, and
      the answer to prayer.
The story seldom changes.
Of every ten who come
    asking for Your help,
generally there's only one —
    if that many! —
who thinks enough to thank You for it.

It's that way at home too,
    isn't it, Lord?
Love is lavished freely
    and truly enjoyed.
But how often do we stop
    to thank for it?

Why, Lord?
We don't do that to strangers.
    For any little favor they do us
      we deluge them
    with expressions of gratitude.
But when it comes to those
    who do the most for us,

we just take
    and take again,
with barely a grunt of gratitude.

Our thanks to You
    is but a small percent
        of our petitions for Your love.
Our thanks to our loved ones
    is usually rather sparse too.

Don't let us take each other
    for granted, Lord!
When one loves enough to give,
    let the other love enough to thank.

False Pride

Who are we, Lord Jesus Christ,
    to be so impressed with ourselves?
What right have we
    to airs of superiority?

Perhaps we have been able to reach
    a higher level of attainment
        than many others around us.
Surely we have cause
    to be genuinely happy
        and excited about it.

Everybody loves the sweet smell
    of success.

But, Lord, let me remember
    I owe full thanks to You
        for what I am
        and what I have.
There is no call to feel smugly superior.

How often I forget to ask,
    "What if . . . ?"
What if I had not been born
    in a land of unlimited opportunity?
What if I had not had access
    to a good education?

What if my health had failed?
What if I had been held back
    by jealous superiors?

How much control have I had
    over such factors?
Is not Your hand of blessing
    evident every step of the way?
"By the grace of God
    I am what I am."

As I look at You, blessed Lord,
    I am touched by Your attitude.
None of us will ever be like You —
    the almighty Son of God.

None of us is like You —
    sinless, perfect.
None of us will ever do what You did —
    save all mankind.

Yet You walked humbly,
    but we oft strut in pride.

Lord Christ, give me
    Your mind and heart.

Indecision

Heavenly Father, I can just feel
    how exasperated Elijah must have been,
    when he thundered:
"How long halt ye
    between two opinions?
If the Lord be God, follow Him!"
When people play around
    with such important decisions,
it's enough to drive anyone
    out of his mind.

Father, give me the ability
    to weigh and evaluate pros and cons,
    and then make a right decision.

Don't let me be the reed
        that bends with the wind.
Don't let me slip into the rut.
        of changing my tune
to please whoever is nearest me
        at the moment.
Help me make up my mind
        and then have the courage
                to stick with it.

Moreover, Father,
        keep me from making
                shallow, snap decisions
and from becoming
        a stubbornly opinionated man.

There must be many times
        when I frustrate You, Father,
much as those people did
        in Elijah's day.
I call and consider myself
        a Christian,
yet I do not always follow You —
        really and truly follow You.

Father, provide me
        with enough wisdom and truth
that I can make good
        and proper decisions.
And when I've made them,
        let me be wholehearted,
                not halfhearted,
                        in sticking to them.

Disagreements

Father, when two people occupy
    differing points of vantage,
there will be many times
    when they see things differently.

It would be virtually impossible,
    when there are dissimilarities
        in sex, role,
    background, and training,
for them to see everything eye to eye.

When divergent views become evident
    in our home, Lord,
show us how to use them
    to good advantage.

So often we make the mistake
    of storming the field.
With a loud and heavy volley of words,
    we try to batter the opposition,
    overcome the resistance,
    and win the day.

Lord, can I really be so foolish?
Is it really so important
    to win an argument?
Or even to argue
    in the first place?

To gain a point
     at the risk of losing
a measure of love and respect?

I marvel at my Savior!
When Jesus was confronted by those
     who would use words to ensnare,
          to belittle or disprove,
oh, how He lashed out,
     putting them in their place
          with well-chosen words!
But how patiently and gently
     and quietly He spoke
when He faced those with honest hearts!
They had their faulty ideas too.
But Jesus won them over
     with words of truth and love.

Father, show me how to approach
     disagreements in that way.
Keep me mindful that I am mere man,
     not like my perfect Lord.
While I desire to win my wife
     to my point of view,
help me to remember —
     she may be right!

Quiet Time

Times do not change very much,
    do they, Lord Jesus?

How often I've felt like Your disciples
    when, as it says of them,
"Many were coming and going,
    and they had no leisure
        even to eat."
That's often been the story
    of my life, Lord!
In fact it usually is!

That's why, Lord Jesus,
    the words that You spoke then
strike such a responsive note in me.

"Come away by yourselves to a lonely place,
    and rest a while," You said.
And You invited them
    to join You on a boat
        and sail away.
Off You glided quietly
    to some place where You could be
        alone together.

O Lord, how much I need
    such quiet times.

Not just I —
    the whole family!
How much we need
    to slip quietly away,
far from the maddening throng,
    far from the hurried pace,
far from the tyranny of telephone —

to be alone —
    all alone together,
    all alone with You.

We need time to think.
    The world affords
        little opportunity for this.
At the rapid rate things happen.
    one can usually do little more
        than observe and note.
We need time to ask ourselves,
    "What does this all mean to us?"
    "What should it mean?"

We need time to be distracted
    from the daily human drama;
to be distracted
    by the thunderclap of a giant wave,
        the rustle of a leaf,
the stateliness of a redwood,
    the majesty of a mountain thrust, or
the quiet of the desert,
    where stars were never more brilliant.

These too have their message
    as they point to Your power and glory.

We need time to pray.
    Too often our daily conversations with You
        are catch-as-catch-can.
In the time apart
    we find ourselves less inclined
        to rush our prayers and
more inclined to ponder
    what You have revealed to us.

We need our quiet times, Lord!
    We need them as a family.
There's real blessing
    in being alone together.

Synthetic Escape

Father, there's so much tension
    in the world around us.

Sometimes it seems the only way out
    is to look for temporary relief —
        some form of synthetic relaxation.
That's why some have turned to alcohol
    and others started using drugs.

There's such a temptation
    to look for help
        where there is no help —
    no help,
        only more problems.

There's such deception in thinking
    that momentary oblivion
        is a form of relief.
It's no relief,
    just a postponement.
Not a strengthening,
    but a weakening of oneself.
One cannot hide in a bottle
    without eventually drowning.

Don't let me get into the habit
    of running away, Father.
For most often, if I'd be wise enough,
    I'd see I'm not really running away
        from my problems.
I'm running away from myself
    and from You.

Give me strength
    to face up to things.
Until I can and do,
    my problems will only rise up
        to haunt me another day.

Give me an undiluted faith,
    a complete confidence in You.

Instead of trying to hide from You
    in embarrassment
        over my inabilities,
    let me turn to You for help.
When I don't, I am like those
    whom You described so well:
"The sound of a shaken leaf
    shall put them to flight . . . .
They shall flee . . . and fall
    when none pursues."

Why should I be "fearful"
    and of "so little faith"?
Why should I run away
    when You are with me?
Can I deem You inadequate
    to help me now in this,
when, for me, in Christ,
    You've already routed hell
        and wrought my eternal redemption?
Could I doubt Your love?
    Could I doubt Your power?

The Bridled Tongue

Lord, why do we men think that gossip
    is primarily confined to the opposite sex?

Aren't we just as prone
        to talk about those around us —
            those with whom we work,
                even our families?

Your Word told us:
    "I will guard my ways,
        that I may not sin with my tongue;
    I will bridle my mouth . . . ."
Lord, help me bridle my tongue!

Let no one reject You
    and all You stand for
because of what they hear from me
    or what they see in me.
Nor let me say anything
    that will hurt others.
At work so often there are insinuations
    and a sparring of words
        whenever a promotion is in the air
            or something has gone wrong.
It's so easy to mouth a rumor —
    so hard to silence it
        or to heal the wound it inflicted.

Lord, there are days
    when even a close husband and wife
        can have their differences.
It takes only a little misunderstanding
    or absent-minded preoccupation
        or varying opinions to bring it on.

Don't let me join the ranks
    of the boys who are always telling tales
        about what happens at home;
    who spill it all out,
        with reluctant willingness,
    to the pleasant and understanding
        (also attractive) girl at work.

Lord, help me to bridle my tongue,
    especially where my loved ones are con-
    cerned.
Keep me so mindful of their love
    that I never have even
        the slightest inclination
            to talk behind their backs.

Let my every word and act
    show how much I really think of them.
Let my every word and act
    also show how much You mean to me.

Friends

Day in, day out, Father,
    it's one superficial contact
        after another.

Just another name,
     another face,
          another voice on the telephone.
Who needs them?

I don't doubt that most of them
     would prove to be pretty fine people
were I to have the chance
     to know them more intimately.
But who wants it?

Living as we are in masses,
     it is inevitable
that most of our associations with others
     remain rather loosely knit.
But, Father, don't ever let me lose sight
     of the blessing that lies
          in having a true friend.

I pray so very much
     that I will ever have a real friend —
someone with whom I can dare
     to be myself,
someone whom I can trust
someone who would be willing
     to go out on a limb for me,
someone who would care enough
     to ease my burden,
someone who would rejoice
     in my good fortune
          and stick with me when I need him most,

someone with open ear
and closed mouth.

I know I can't expect perfection
in any friend.
I can find that only in You, Lord.
"Greater love has no man than this,
that a man lay down his life
for his friends."
Jesus did that for me,
for my eternal salvation,
as my never-failing Friend.

Make me, in turn,
a loyal, trustworthy friend too.

In Time of Sickness

As I lie here, Father,
feeling quite sorry for myself,
I have an unusually good chance
to do a little serious thinking.

When things go well day after day,
if I remember,
I give thanks to You
for all the obvious blessings.

99

In days like these,
  when aches and fever conspire
    to disrupt routine,
I am inclined to limit my prayers
  to pleas and petitions.

Show me that this is also a time
  for praise and thanks, Father.

Do not my moments of weakness
  awaken me to Your power?
Do not my bouts with illness
  confront me with Your healing love?
Is it not in hours like these
  that You draw me closer to You
    and strengthen my faith?
Is it not at times like these
  that You untangle my perspective
    and allow me to see clearly
  what is truly important
    and what is not?

So I ask, Father, that,
  if it be in accord
    with Your loving will,
You grant the return
  of health and strength.

But I ask also that,
  while You are working this out
    in terms of Your schedule,
You give me patience and peace.

Peace — in knowing Your presence
    and trusting Your love and power.
Patience — to see the blessing in each day,
        just as it comes,
            and to be content
                and grateful for it.

Buying a Home

What a happy time, Lord!

A man dreams of the day
    when he can buy his own home —
a place where he can stretch his arms
    and relax contentedly;
where his wife can give free play
    to all her artistic touches;
where the children can have sun and air
    and plenty of space to play.

Thank You, Father,
    for the dream fulfilled.

It is a little frightening at first,
    when you hear of mortgage,
        decades of payments,
    and unrelenting taxes.

But it is ours,
    increasing in value
as we constantly pour
    fresh love and care into it.

Bless our home, Lord,
    from the moment we enter it.

Keep us mindful
    that the true strength
        of our home
lies not in its concrete foundation,
    its beams and joists,
        or skillful framing.
Its true beauty is not found
    in its textured walls,
        its natural-grained cabinetry
    its copious use of glass and tile.

What makes a house
    a strong and beautiful home
is the material of which
    its occupants are made.

Love can transform
    the most modest home
        into an Eden.
Faith can make
    even a lowly dwelling
        a secure fortress.

Lord, look in favor on our home.
Fill it with joy and blessing
    peace and comfort.
Abide with us in it.
May it be as much Your home
    as ours.

Just One Last Word

Just one last word, Lord —
    and I can confine it to one word —
        "Thanks!"

    Thank You for life —
        her life,
        my life,
        our life in Christ.
    Thank You for love —
        Your love,
        her love.
    Thank You for marriage —
        companionship,
        oneness in purpose,
        togetherness in result.
    Bless our marriage —
        today and
        through all the years to come.

Bless us with Your presence.
Bless us with peace,
    hope,
    joy,
    tenderness —
in short, with all those blessings
    that You willed to be a part of marriage
      since the very beginning.